MW00488480

FINISHING LINE PRESS
www.finishinglinepress.com

Revolutions We'd Hoped We'd Outgrown

poems by

Jill McCabe Johnson

Finishing Line Press
Georgetown, Kentucky

Revolutions We'd Hoped We'd Outgrown

ISBN 978-1-63534-076-1 First Edition

ACKNOWLEDGMENTS

Thank you to the editors of the following publications where these poems first appeared:

Barely South Review: "Horseshoe Highway"
Floating Bridge Review: "Honey, it's raining something terrible," "Kitchen Waltz"
Help Wanted anthology: "First Kill"
Iron Horse Literary Review: "Apple Tree"
miller's pond: "Winter Letter," Winter 2010
Moonglasses Magazine, "Where Did You Go?"
Oak Bend Review: "Lunar Sea"
Orcas Issues: "Favorite Theater," "North Beach, Low Tide"
Poetry Quarterly: "What I Think about When Trying not to Think about our Argument Last Night," "Escape"
Rock & Sling: "Stained Glass"
Sea Stories: "Sleep Song"
Sweet Anthology: "Berries, late summer"
Shark Reef: "Saying Goodbye," "Snag"
Third Wednesday: "Their Car the Day After"
Fire on Her Tongue: "A Course around the Garden," "Sea Urge from Nebraska"
An Expression of Depression anthology: "But I'm walking now"
Umbrella: "The Abscess Absence of Paranoia"
Windfall: A Journal of Poetry of Place: "Alula"

Publisher: Leah Maines

Editor: Christen Kincaid

Cover Art: AdobeStock_102665635.jpeg

Author Photo: Charles Toxey

Printed in the USA on acid-free paper.
Order online: www.finishinglinepress.com
also available on amazon.com

Author inquiries and mail orders:
Finishing Line Press
P. O. Box 1626
Georgetown, Kentucky 40324
U. S. A.

Table of Contents

WHO FIDGET IN THEIR PEWS WAITING

FOR THAT SLOW CRAFTED BARGAIN WITH TIME

TO EASE OUR LOSS DOWN GENTLY

To my family, given and chosen.
You are precious beyond words.

WITH EACH MINDLESS STEP

Marche a l'Arc de Triomphe

Paris, October 19, 2015

The girls on ponies in Parc Monceau
were more interested in you taking their picture
than in the park's round-the-world follies
or even the carousel with its dead and decorated mounts.

The children wore hairnets like gossamer armor
between rented helmets and diminutive heads.
Their ennui as genuine as the underwhelmed
hands lying limp in their laps.

Did each child beg, *please may I ride a pony?*
The instinct to connect with animus—
to encircle and tame with one's legs—
a primitive and innocent, as yet, impulse.

Of course, those girls had outgrown the carousel
with its slow circle of horses, looping accordion music,
and even the bellows of their own breaths, rising
and falling in a predictable slog.

Every revolution ripe for advantage—
just as Napoleon ransacked the runnels
of his wearied warriors, or Daesh in the wake
of Arab Spring, or as children will consume

each small victory. Fuel for the next execution
of accomplishment. Who understands hunger
better than the hapless child hankering
for power and control. Even the hoped for thrill

of danger, the compulsion toward beastly mounts,
disappoints with each round-the-park trudge.
We aim the camera elsewhere as canter and clomp
trail away, and I think, *Syria's knocking at the border,*

while we gaze at facsimiles of Renoir's Dance at Bougival.
We turn like clumsy dancers ourselves, or trained ponies
galumphing in pace with the other people-ponies.
Our slow circuit no more nimble than this traffic-clogged

paradise for dead heroes and Napoleon's monument
to revolutions we'd hoped we'd outgrown.

Tramping the Quai du Canal
Esbly, October, 27, 2015

I.
Hedges of yew,
their berries the luminous
color of currants,
and the towering, priestly
hemlock in his raiment,
fingers pointing *a ciel.*
Such treacherous poisons,
they always dress
in the promising colors of *la vie*,
the everlasting scent of *miel.*

II.
Church bells ripple
unhindered over water,
the sound at once
as comforting and constraining
as the illusion
of Euclidean space
and all the other ways
we tell ourselves we're safe.

III.
Distant poplars quiver in sunlight,
and a thousand citrine glimmers
shower off the leaves to echo
along the water's surface,
like the chorus and applause
for Hamlet's final soliloquy.
All winter we cry:
Encore! Encore!
as October's final
curtain falls.

We Walk

Montry, October 30, 2015

We walk and feel the stubble and duff
of the ground through flimsy soles—

feet pressing, caressing each nub
and divot masked by grass—

and believe by this tendering
we know the earth better,

though we can never know it fully.
We carry it with us the muck and mud

the dew that skirts the hems of our pants.
We carry its story and scent in pockets

and crevices, under fingernails, hidden
in the murmurs of private incantations.

Foolishly, we watch it extending
behind us with each mindless step

as though the world turns at our discretion.
The horizon tumbles away

outside our purview and we cobble
a tale that all that lies past

the imagination doesn't exist.
When we walk this world blindly

we pretend the cultured landscape
can be named natural,

while what we call wildness
lives only in the imagination.

The true nature we resist is nothing
more than our own undoing:

the honeyed fragrance of decomposing
leaves and journey and song.

On the Hazards of Walking
Esbly, October 31, 2015

The passenger pelts a wild, swinging *Hallooooo* for
my benefit, and the shockwave of his voice, its wholesale
assault, hits me and the aftershock of *Babyeeeee*!
judders through me—scalp, fingertips, even through my shoes
to the hard ground and back up my shins. I'll never
see his face, nor confront him, and definitely not get used

to how men like that have hollered and abused
the privilege of being allowed out in public for
as long as anyone can remember. Sailors
& soldiers, jerks & jocks, and does it start as a baby,
crying hungry in the crib, begging to suck and chew
on mommy's magic globe of milk? Do they never

get enough of the sustenance they drain from us, never
figure out that when they yell *Titties*! no one is amused?
As kids, my sister and I walked through the woods for
a shortcut home from school when we were assailed
by some guy winking the sheen off his purple baby
wee-wee and we ran as fast as our little saddle shoes

could carry us. The thing is a child can't just shoo
off an experience like that. Jenelle and I could never
walk in those woods, into any woods without the bruise
of dread making us queasy or quake. And not for
fear of some putz priming himself for the swale
of his own exhibition, but because we'd been made babes

in the woods, who, at best would hear *Hey, baby*
from some clueless and swaggering excuse
of a boyfriend, and at worst, get dragged down an ever
more terrifying trail of abduction, abuse,
rape, torture, and/or death. So when guys laugh or
snicker over supposedly harmless cat-calling I want to say

let those men endure the firestorm assault
of demeaning, derogatory, and daily *Oooh babys!*
If they too lived with the threat of rape shoved
up their psyches, would they know what it's like to never
feel safe walking home? Of course, I can't blame them because
not every man is a catcaller or rapist. Still, we've said it before:

Women are not squeaky toys or cupcakes at a bake sale.
And we are definitely not mindless baby-makers. Walk in our shoes.
We are your sisters on the trail. We never asked to be used.

March of La Toussaint

Seine et Marne, November 1, 2015

The trail bears the tread of bicycle churn.
Its broken loam and clay molds to the tamp
of my boot soles whose hiking in turn
the trail must bear.

In France, La Toussaint is the day of the dead,
when families brave the cold air and damp
to place flowers on loved ones' grave beds.

My brother Mark, at age ten, built a bicycle ramp
near the end of the driveway. He raced and sped,
then airborne, at age 56, torqued a one-eighty like a champ.

But now, as families flood the cemeteries outside
Paris—Mark's old stomping grounds—I tramp
tethered and writhing on the path to the dead.

We've long since scattered his ash-filled urn,
and I, wearied from writer's cramp and regrets,
walk miles in the hopes that my gravest concerns
surely the trail can bear.

Winter Crop

Paris suburb, November 7, 2015

Walking alone in a country where I don't speak the language,
I stop when a van pulls onto the gravel shoulder ahead.
The solitary driver cuts his engine, then watches me in his side mirror.
I cross the road just as a cyclist rounds the curve, and the van departs.

To my left, acres of fields sleep under mulch, to my right, the first shoots
of a winter crop rise from agitated earth. I'm four or five kilometers
into my trip, uncertain how much farther to the train. As the sun spills
from the horizon, thousands of spider webs glow: a cocoon of golden filaments.

Another cyclist whirs by, and my tired legs can almost feel
the smooth ease of gears and motion as the rider breezes past.
I never learned to ride a bike. My parents couldn't afford one for me.
I used to wonder if it was because I was a girl, but I know now I'm lucky.

In much of the world, girls get little to no education, their fate
(determined by religious extremists) to mate and mother and mourn.
Michele Obama brings books and pressure to the Middle East
while Boko Harem stockpiles a battery of short-range missiles.

When newspapers report that *Daesh* instructs soldiers to gang rape
the girls they abduct, that repeated assaults will make them Muslim,
I think of how many religions expect their women to lie prostrate
and receive the punishing planting of seed and enslavement.

I want to run up and down every row of that cold winter crop,
my legs strong, my feet powerful—powerful enough to tear apart
the networks of webs that lie in wait to entrap and devour
their slowly dying prey. The world teems with desperate hungers.

But I throw back my shoulders and stride briskly to the train.
I honestly don't know how we women should arm ourselves,
with books or bombs? With compassion or contempt?
What I do know is a woman should be able to walk,
safe and strong, to rise up, and reach her rightful station.

Walking to the Gare

Magny-le-Hongre, November 8, 2015

Everywhere leaves skydive, spinning and twisting,
head-over-stems in a freefall as forsythia,
primroses, and azaleas bloom their second spring.

Walking alongside rue Berthe Morisot, I step
over clover, wood anemone, and wild strawberry flowers
whose perfume makes promises it cannot keep.

A calandra lark lifts off its grassy nest and weaves
wings and flight into a moving song of summer passed
and the harsh winter icing across the horizon.

I savor the mélange of wood smoke, rotting leaves,
and still-pulsing, caramel notes of sequoia and cedar—
once more drawn to the lure of thrum, blossom, and burn.

La Légende des Siècles
Paris, November 10, 2015

Stopping on the way to Charles de Gaulle,
I climb the stairs from the Metro to Les Halles

to use the bathroom at Starbucks, and find a band
of semi-automatic wielding gendarmes.

At the airport, police and military personnel
practically outnumber the passengers

and when I wander the first arrondissement,
I encounter more armed militia

in small groups, eyeing the crowds carefully.
Notre Dame. The Eiffel Tower. The only

places I don't see them are northern districts
like Le Marais where I visit the Maison de Victor

Hugo, who wrote his poem for Muhammad's
Hegira, when the self-proclaimed prophet fled

Mecca after being warned of an assassination plot,
and slipped away before the planned onslaught.

Wall of the Centuries

Dordogne, November 13-14, 2015

We strap on packs to time travel
on the *Grande Randonnée,* following
the route of pilgrims and poets
of the *Moyen Âge*, singing
our song of adventure. Escaping

the crowds of Paris. Live
oaks scatter acorns, while
thousand-year-old stone roofs
remind us the earth is ready
to outlive us all. A collie leads us

to truffles and the traditional
dinner of the Dordogne,
goose liver, duck, *salade*
Perigorde. We hobble through
smatterings of French, murdering

the language with our ignorance.
It isn't until the next morning
we learn the news: Daesh attacks
in Paris, some just blocks from
where we had walked and dined

at sidewalk cafés. A concert,
we learn, in French is called
a *spectacle*, but we shield our eyes
from what the television shows us,
what Daesh wants us to see. Death

is a blanket, covering the ground,
muting everything. We walk
the somber steps to Castelnaud,
stare across the valley of the
Hundred Years War. Fog

filters the slow sun and we
imagine we can stand behind
ramparts to detect an enemy's
approach, to protect France, Syria,
and all the people and places we love.

En Paris, où je suis né

San Antonio, November 30, 2015

Tourists queue for hot chocolate at Angelina's

Men stand at counters, arguing and sipping café

Joanna Walsh reads from *Vertigo* at Shakespeare & Company

Mistletoe dangles in black poplars

Mums fade at impromptu memorials

180 world leaders talk climate change

Thousands of empty shoes stand in for *Paris en Marche*

Children savor roasted chestnuts on rue de Rivoli

Accordionists sing *Le Foule* in the Metro

And the moon circles over the Seine

New York, Beirut, Damascus, Paris, Baghdad, Brussels, and Here

Saratoga, March 22, 2016

News of the attacks erupted across the wires.
At 3 am, I woke to a feed exploding with pictures

of windows framed in broken glass, the ground thick
and spattered with the stunned, prone, and panicked.

Troops coalesced while the rest of the world coped
as we always do, fighting religion with religion, trope

with cliché, peril with prayer. Here in the mountains,
when snow fell we mistook it for peace and sat silenced—

as rapt at the window as we'd sat at the screen—lifted
and comforted by simple flakes. The snow drifted

though, the way ash floats in the deafened aftermath
of every fanatic's flame and firebomb, rant and wrath.

Ni Putes, Ni Soumises

Neither Sluts, Nor Submissives

1. Joan of Arc

Only by God's dictate delivered in a dream
was she allowed to mount a horse and lead
the army that swept through France's foreign invaders.
Armored and armed, she donned men's clothes
to charge with the tattered and ragtag
French militia across the redoubts
where the British had dared to settle
French soil. After the farce of a trial,
where she swore her allegiance
to God's divine word and mission,
the Brits torched Joan at the stake—
once, twice, then, to make sure, thrice—
though not for the courage to defend her lands,
but having the audacity to act like a man.

2. Lady Godiva

On a bet with her husband to free tenants from taxes
she rode nude from one end of town to the other,
while residents remained indoors, backs to windows,
with the exception of the prurient Peeping Tom.
Did our lady coil her hair to cover breasts
and bottom, or pitch forward so the horse's neck
could shield her vulnerability? Did she lead
a dignified canter or gallop so fast the mare's
mane lifted in wind to cover her courageous ride?
And how did she manage the daily negotiations
of a marriage where nakedness was her only power,
she who lived in a time when woman were property—
childbearing vessels whose virtue was gauged by
virginal status or number of healthy sons?

3. Fadela Amara

When a seventeen year old girl was burned alive
by her friends and family for some supposed
infraction of feminine surrender, Fadela led
the march of protest. Maybe the girl wore makeup
or let slip a lock of her hair. Maybe she took flight
in the tender kisses of a lover. Maybe she'd been raped.
And what is honor really? The promise of supreme
and unrelenting submission? Dishonor apparently
is not the murder of one's sister, cousin, daughter, friend.
Even if she had been raped, forced to sacrifice
her only recognized worth, by Sharia law
her testimony would be valued at exactly half
of a man's—not even a standoff of her word
against his—and her life worth even less.

YOU MIGHT BE DRUMMING UP THE NERVE

Sleep Song

If whales can find themselves in the wrong passage,
directionless, swimming in their sleep, then who is to say
we are not floating in our own slumber, years into emptiness
with nothing but the day-in, day-out sway.

Combing through tide-swept marriages, we pluck remnants:
The strewn toys, refrigerator schedules, plans to go camping,
and the promise of a second honeymoon ebbed.
Whales do travel in their sleep. Passive echolocation

alerts them to rocks, ships, lost jobs, and the rank wounds
of the disgruntled dear. We sleep in front of the television.
We disregard tsunami tremors and the salt-stained traces
of desolation. No wonder whales beach themselves.

No wonder they linger in the receding tide
of whatever luck has carried them this far
but now leaves them languishing
amid driftwood and broken shells.

Cavity

All I know is if you're skinny and some girl
bigger than you are steals your purse,

there's not a thing you can do to stop her.
You might chase after her, which is all she wants,

or you can act tough, saying, *keep the damn thing,*
there's nothing in it worth having anyway.

You might be sitting on a hill just outside
the Business Ed wing of your high school.

It would be summer, the school deserted,
and you weighing your mother's advice

to take typing so you'll always have a job
in the secretarial pool. You might be drumming

up the nerve to tell your mom you're going
to study French instead. The girl swings your purse

then one-by-one tosses out your lip gloss, mascara,
and whatever else you carry to look grown up.

There will always be someone bigger than you.
There will always be someone lonelier, too.

When the girl holds up your half-empty
pack of cigarettes, saying, *I'm keeping these,*

then hurls the bag back at you, her loneliness
will penetrate where the purse strikes, lodging

in your chest cavity another twenty or thirty years.
You'll stub out your last cigarette, pull at the grass,

and in September you will drop out of typing
and enroll in French without saying a word
to your mother or anyone else for that matter.

A Course around the Garden

He wrested foliage from a rhubarb stalk
and fanned himself with the blood-veined leaf.

Pretend someone murdered your son, he said.

He plucked blossoms from the foxglove
to encase my fingers' ends.

What would you do for revenge?

He stroked the umbel flowers, carved
a whistle from water hemlock's stem.

I guess I would rely on the judicial system, I said.

He fingered the coral beads on my necklace,
spoke of rosary peas tainted black.

What would you do, I asked him, *if you wanted revenge?*

He stepped through jack-in-the-pulpit's
low, triangulated heart.

Execution can easily look like an accident...

He led me into belladonna's
dusk of deadly nightshade.

...but I would let nature take its slow course.

The ~~Abscess~~ Absence of Paranoia

The fern feathered across the top of your latte is
        ~~not a sign, nor is it~~
an arrow pointing out strangers in the alley.

My son's action figures
        ~~strewn across the floorboards of the car don't~~
have a message for you.

Your toothache is merely
        ~~a toothache, despite the urgency of searing pain. Abscess is not~~
a vehicle the gods use to reveal their multifarious plans.

The encyclopedia of symbols and your secret decoder ring
        ~~can't help you. Only you~~
have the answers. Today before you

lock the doors, pull the
        ~~blinds, and hide, remember, fear is your~~
trigger. Only you can end the pain.

What I Think About When Trying Not to Think About Our Argument Last Night

Angle of glacier to tundra, 10,000 years separated into striations of cells frozen in purgatory
as we wait for wheat to acquiesce, hay to limbo, billows and bales roiling across the plain
candy and frilled confections posed in a pageant of hard-stripe ribbon at the sweet shop mercantile
turnstile still costs a penny to ride, enter the big tent and gawk from behind a rope at Siamese
twin towers a snowfall, hammer-tap avalanche, sifting from the ascension of smoke
signals the right track for the afternoon train, temporary obstruction, what slices land connects
lovers back to back, waiting to breach, to swallow, these tangible channels of churning air

Sarah's Chord Progressions

Your 12-string leans against the end of the sofa
and thrums a drowsy midnight when I press you
to play. *In California,* you say, *there is no winter.*

The sun shines brighter than orange
juice at the organic bakery and it's warm in January,
not like Portland, not like how we read the paper
and eat our Sunday scones.

Even though the barista wears fringed boots
and under her bangs a henna design
her boyfriend took one look at
and said, *Take that shit off,*
she calls her feelings love.

There's a new Alejandro Amenábar
at the Laurelhurst tonight, or we could just stay in,
stream some movie on Netflix
about grieving widows or a romance
on the brink, eat microwave popcorn
and basically chill.

When we unfurl from our tangle on the sofa
but before we ratchet down our love,
you'll wedge your guitar behind the door
to the spare bedroom, now yours, and ladle
scoop after scoop of chocolate peanut-butter bliss
while I scarf down a full bag of jalapeño chips.
I never eat like this.

Sure, we'll stay friends, but after six months apart,
please don't call to say you're training for a triathlon
or taking Spanish guitar from the virtuoso
you met at yoga and how finally you've been able
to pursue your passions without me holding you back,
because we both know there's a difference
between filling the fallow hours
and following a dream.

Nova

1.

The first time, Led Zeppelin swirled
against water-stained sheetrock,
and you tugged at my hand, hanging
loose like a thread waiting to be unraveled.
You pulled me outside
where your lips sang silently
of that secret love the sky saves
for the meadow. And what if
I thought tiny stars cascaded
in waterfalls over my limbs,
and the broken hinge of our bodies
tasted like bliss wrapped in thin foil?
Would you have mocked
my naiveté, the delicate skin
of pears, how easily it tears?

2.

The second and only other time,
you took me back to your apartment,
where you poured something clear—
tequila, vodka, rum, gin? The memory
hides from itself certain transgressions,
scalds the rest under a faucet of recriminations,
like how I let you rift me from the sofa, carry me,
onto that wide expanse of silken sheets,
a lake of vague hopes
that you and I would be boyfriend and girlfriend,
promise rings and the prom.
But oh how your hands
covered my mouth, squeezed
at my throat, pillow over my face,
my own hands flailing,
and the choking, afterward
coughing and coughing,
tremors and the taste of rust
that scuppered and scuffed me for months.

3.

I heard about your death
some twenty years later,
a high school reunion or coffee
with your younger sister, she herself
just barely back from one addiction
or another. When she mentioned heroin,
I wondered if it smoldered like the scorched coursing
in my veins when we first kissed,
and I grieved that your passions
sought only destruction. Your poor sister
who later had to explain to all her friends
that you had picked us off, one-by-one,
that the gravitational power of your older-boy appeal
was matched only by your gravitational pull toward collapse,
that stardust is just the sift
of dried and drifting cinders,
that we'd sacrificed our first time
for a taste of love you could never offer to a woman,
and never accept from a man.
Eventually, HIV turned to AIDS.
Your slender body
became a haphazard facsimile
fashioned from desiccated beetles, cobwebs,
and bits of frayed thread.

4.

Astrophysicists say the white dwarf
has such a gravitational pull
that if a companion star comes close enough
the white star will accrete gases and small
lengths of inconsequential string
until it torches itself in a blinding blaze.
Sometimes, in binary systems, the gases will fall
into a kind of tear-shaped mass
like when we danced at your wedding
and you, drunk not with love, whispered
how you dreaded entering the bridal chamber,
and asked me not to stop dancing. Never
to stop dancing. I side-stepped
your two-step to drag the other dancers
into our lopsided but ever-expanding
circle of combustible gases.

5.

I used to go back
and look for ways I should have known
I was too young or too ugly
to deserve genuine affection,
that awkward girls like me
don't get invited to the prom.
For years I believed I had a paper bag
kind of face, so hideous
you had to bury it and pretend (as I had done)
that I could be someone you actually wanted.
Who knew you were hiding,
if not my prettiness, then the feminine gloss
painted on lips, cheeks, and lashes
leaving only my boyish body in view.
Funny how I never blamed you.
After all, everyone knows it's always the girl's fault,
even when it isn't. But I guess I thought
the betrayal of my body in pleasure
deserved the betrayal of your body in control.
Now I go back and look for ways
I could have seen your secret
love the sky saves for the sky.
I was fourteen.
What did I know about anything.
A hand reaching for a hand.
A hand covering a mouth.
A hand at a throat.
Maybe mine, maybe some other girl's.
Maybe your own.

Birds at the Bon Odori Festival

August delivers fresh sun and sky
as the four of us prance in cotton,
hand-me-down kimonos. Our flat,
round fans chop the air in jagged
choreography. We can't feel
our clumsiness until after the dance
when we sit at the edge of the grass,
outside the temple, to watch
our older sisters, and then our mothers,
perform with small, restrained movements
and humble grace. The silk fans spread
like a monarch's wings, curved
coyly in front of their bodies.

Their heads turn shyly toward the shoulder.
and lift in time to shield telltale traces
of smiles. Under the swollen sun
and breathless sky we see each flock
rising in turn from a single oak tree
to sweep and carve the air
before lighting on limbs to view
the next flock. We become aware
of chirping as the birds observe
each other practicing maneuvers,
preparing for their autumn flight.

The shadows of birds flutter over grass.
They dance with shadows of our mothers'
fans while we practice with our own
crude fans, we four girls,
perched as we are on the edge.

LIKE THE CROWS IN THE BRANCHES ABOVE

Apple Tree

The last summer he gardened, our father trained an espalier
to sprout wings along the fence where it could catch sunlight
arcing across the horizon. We knew eventually he would leave.

We knew even his recorded voice answering Mom's phone now—
We're sorry we missed your call. We're not home at the moment.
—would no longer startle us. I used to stand

in front of the apples and leaves, listening to windchimes
Dad had constructed from spoons and scrap metal. Dad's voice,
Please leave a message —prompting us, reassuring us—at the tone.

Saying Goodbye

And if I loved you, I could say, stay with me. —Istvan Laszlo Geher

Another day in a city of days
where the sun doles light,
and work numbs like a jigger of gray,

gray as the sidewalk where we walk.
Where maple leaves
filter brightness in metered doses of green.

And if a crow lay motionless
but for the tremor of her wings,
would we not curb our wretchedness,

like the crow's mate in the branches above,
who protects his beloved
from the early grief in his call?

But no, the bird in the tree cries simply, *stay with me,*
and our sidewalk crow,
crippled and scarred, answers, *stay.*

A Thin Parade of Ants

after Naomi Shihab Nye, in memoriam Gerald Shapiro

Each steps
into the footfall
of his predecessor,
a winnowing of will—
this learning to follow,
this learning to fall.

Dark matter
is the mulch we tread,
a step and another.
When the willow offers
her long strands of sorrow
to the breeze,
who is it who cries,
the wind or the tree?

Once, when we sat around
a table such as this,
you told your students
I am not your friend.
I love you,
but I am not your friend,
and I grieved.

We filed out of the classroom,
ant after ant,
and you led the way,
confessing, *Tonight*
I will lie awake
in the scant hours of doubt
and listen to the clock
recount my failures.

Gerry, I cling
to branches and wind
as though the ground
were a long way down.

Snag

I put Mom to bed, frail as a torn rag,
and tried to forget her rickety legs
at the edge of the chair, my hands under her bony seat,
her shoulders fretting against mine
as I lifted her hips to standing,
the way she rested her head against my neck,
and I could feel the rattle, chest to chest,
of her fractured breathing.

After pajamas and dentures,
after blankets and a kiss,
I went to the basement where my bed rests,
one floor below hers, perpendicular in attitude,
crosswise, as though I could block where she was going.
It might have been hours before I fell asleep,
but sleep did come because I remember rousing,
lost in night, with only the sound of the wind thrashing the house.

Mom's bedroom took the brunt of it—
violent blasts. Winter blowing through our lives.
Towed into that dark sleep, I felt the wind
slash her besieged body, snag her
tattered breath like a rag borne
into nothingness. All night I chased after it,
searching branches and twigs, desperate to retrieve
her frayed and threadbare breath.

But I'm walking now

In these awful hours I put one idle hand
into the pocket of a jacket so long neglected
I can't remember the last time I hid inside it.
Probably a day like today when the clouds lean close.

I gauge the gravel under my feet to assure myself
the dead are really gone, despite no funeral procession.
Out of respect, I decide to keep my car lights on,
for a year, maybe more. But I'm walking now.

One hand is attached to the dog's leash,
while the other rummages through emptiness,
and I think I imagine the debris of a broken cigarette
working its way into my coat pocket's seams.

It's been two months since I let my mother down in death,
walked away when the breathing was at its worst, but more than
twenty years since my last smoke. Still, I taste it, slightly stale and
satisfying in the way failure embraced tastes better than failure imposed.

Mentally I turn off the lights, decide not to flash my grief
and follow the dog instead. *I can do this,* I tell myself.
I can sniff my way forward, nose to the ground.
I can finger the dried leaves of hand-sown damage.
I can slump under imminent skies.

Stained Glass

Lead separates the panes
                    into solitary issues
          of light and fracture

like the way sound travels
                    in a completely different trajectory
          from bullets in a Charleston church.

Methodist, Episcopal, African American:
                    the name of the church defies
          certain segregations,

maintains others. Some people say
                    that when the sun illuminates
          a stained glass window,

the shadow of the lead
                    is the only black visible,
          relegated to the background.

Others say the silhouette
                    frames and forms the image,
          offering strength, shape and substance.

For too long, black
                    has carried those panes—
          the metal malleable and forgiving—

has been asked to stand up
                    to that other, piercing lead,
          asked to hold our

shattered luminescences together.

Encounter

I'm sorry I keep bringing up the family
of raccoons we saw crossing the street,
especially the adolescent that scurried

eight feet up the trunk of a Douglas fir
and peeked his head out to watch us.
I'm sorry I keep reliving the way we

watched back, riveted and marveling
at his paw hands, how easily he clung
to the bark, how the dog, watching too,

never made a sound. So many distractions—
raccoons and dogs and paws and trees
—to keep me from remembering

how once my abdomen did not pool
in discomfiting softness when you placed
your own hand on the trunk of my fears.

I know that, like any good mammal, we can
hold ourselves and our love aloft, but I turn
my head, say how wonderful it was,
that walk when we stared openly
at otherness so unmasked, primal, and near.

Gray Wolf

What thousand things did Lucy smell streaming into her muzzle,
downwind from the wolf? Could she taste the range
of his travels, the rim of the Great Basin riding in his fur?

Rent of consummated packrat, trace of eviscerated vole.
If she tasted gusts of his maleness and it stirred in her
wistful hesitation, we cannot know. It's possible

she was upwind and did not flare her nostrils at his canine otherness,
the musk wafting from glands in his cheeks and anus,
nestled between pads on cracked and calloused toes.

When her human stopped short and silenced her breath,
Lucy's awareness would have doubled. Did she sense
a tinge of fear or smell rabies festering in the blood?

Lucy has it good here by the lake. Her human feeds her
but the ducks and heron, the field mouse and badger
belong to her. The humans belong to her.

Lucy shot toward the wolf, chased him across the highway
and up Winter Ridge as her human called,
Lucy! Lucy! her eyes on the oncoming cars.

I understand the impulse, running heedless,
chasing off danger—tracking what's wild.
How long till the wolf edged his way

down the hillside and back to the pond?
Did he watch Lucy and her human run inside their house?
What thousand things did *his* nose tell *him*

of pheasant, lizard, rattler eggs, kibble, leaves, and dusk
—what loneliness and longing hovered in twilight
after Lucy scampered safely home?

Where did you go?

You remember how I was telling you about my
sister's first apartment in Oakland and the way
the balcony overlooked the swimming pool like
so many apartments did back then, with a pool
instead of a courtyard, so everyone can watch everyone,
well I got to thinking and double-checked and
sure enough, her apartment was on the ground floor!
Not the second story! Can you believe it?
The mind is not to be trusted, I tell you what.
So then I was thinking maybe everything I told you
was messed up: the time I walked into a post at the mall,
and that boss I had who obsessively creased her slacks,
and the 31-Flavors in Burien—the more I think about it,
the more I think it was actually in White Center, which
we used to call Rat City—and god only knows
about the series of labyrinth dreams with the talking puppet,
but dreams are so crazy anyway. Besides,
when I couldn't find you anywhere in the house,
I went looking for you outside because I just had to tell you
about the apartment, and guess what? I saw a quarter
of a feather! There's a story there, what do you want to bet.
I'm not sure what kind of feather it was, wing maybe,
and grayish-white, could've been a seagull or heron or
I don't know, maybe an eagle even, and don't you wish
you could just follow something like that and know
its entire life-story, right down to every detail like
how each feather died, and do feathers die anyway or
are they already dead? Maybe they're completely insensitive
and just feel at the point of attachment, kind of like
a cat's whisker? We should look that up later. Life
is all so fascinating. But first I wanted to tell you about
this car that pulled into the driveway while I was looking
for you, I think the driver was just turning around, but
I got to thinking, what if he was a spy or drug-runner
who went to the wrong address, and we just thought
he was some guy, I mean, that would be really interesting.

We could get killed just because you went outside
and I had to go looking for you, and you never know
what will happen, do you? Hey, do you want to
walk to the store with me? I have this idea for a movie,
sort of a *Bridesmaids* meets *Hunger Games* kind of thing.
I'd love to get your opinion on it, but we don't have to,
I mean, we could just hang out here and that'd be okay,
too, I mean, you know, whatever you want to do.

WHO FIDGET IN THEIR PEWS WAITING

Escape

I should have been a jeweler.
Six months on the coast
selling trinkets to tourists,
six months on another coast
making snake bracelets
in some shanty town where the mind
can follow a trash-lined but glittering
footpath to the beach.

I should have been a fly-fisherman.
Kick off my shoes
and let the earth uncoil
a perfect arcing cry
from my soles through my arm whipping
to the hook end of a hickory pole,
glazed fish dazzled, and slicing
open the incredulous water and sky.

I should have been a priest.
Holiness scattered
with a flick of my fingers,
blessed mist broadcast to masses
who fidget in their pews, waiting
to receive the dangerous sacraments
of communion, confession,
deliverance and grace.

The Myth of the Epic

Ever since the hero's journey
became a blueprint for recruitment,
pastors and politicians have raised their rally cry
to fight, not for change,
but keep things ever the same

until we reach the tipping point,
cause for the next revolution.
But if every revolution roars indignation
against injustice and inequity,
then every revolutionary is a heroine

championing hope, pumping the heart,
blowing air into the deflated lungs
of tomorrow's tomorrow. Everyone
except the campaigner in crusader's clothing,
championing a fight for puffed up ideals,

thumping his chest, blowing hot air
as he calls for every able-bodied dreamer
to sacrifice his life for the latest trumped up
war. Worse yet, is the barter of rights
for reassurances, *we're keeping you*

safe, we've got your back, America,
this so-called greatest country on earth.
And so it goes. Oppression begets revolution.
But revolution begets the window for tyranny,
or at least establishment, which begets more

oppression, which goes on begetting till even
the cycle of revolutions becomes its own revolution
and we're stuck on the spinning carousel, dizzy
and clinging to a wary-go-round of our own making,
afraid of the next rotation and afraid to let go.

Vergelegen

An ache in the gut down deep, farther than the botanical tour
where you walked the cobbled paths of Vergelegen Garden

alongside my brother whose camera rendered into 2-D the expansive
limbs of the yellowwood tree that lives for hundreds of years

where *Vergelegen* means "situated far away." When you visited
seven years ago you said nothing of the pain like a fist

tightening around your fallopian tubes and womb, ovaries
dotted with stage four splotches on test results no one wanted

to believe. *Six months. Maybe*, they said. You swallowed chemo,
like water, bathed your cells for seven flowing years.

Last month you called to say your lymph nodes survived
but your bone marrow faltered. *Weeks, maybe days*, and I turned

my car toward Portland, drove alongside the Columbia River
that carries Hanford's irradiated waste to the sea, and mourned

that tainted desert as though riding alongside your yellowed bones.
Today we talk blood counts. Transfusions have turned days

into weeks, weeks into months, as you make plans for Thanksgiving.
One of these days you or I will die. If I go first, think of me

when you think of rivers, the essence of my life floating ever away.
And if you dive headfirst into that moment we call nothingness, forgive me

if I cannot think of you as gone. Forgive me
if I only think of you as situated far away.

A Place for the Genuine

After Marianne Moore

I understand the resistance to Place—
I, too, dislike it   romanticized, yet even
I am a foreign invader here.
I have projected nothing but self as
I reconstruct my impressions from life, but

we're all guilty of rewriting history.
We shape our cultural schemas based on how
we hope to live in the world we recreate. When
we give a place a name or when
we craft our own names—ISIS, ISIL, Daesh—

you and I both know they're political constructs, but
you use them anyway. In the deficit of anything better,
you make due. Republican. Democrat. Gibbertarian.
You strap yourself onto the party that serves
you, and make a place for yourself at a table

nobody—not me, not you—really believes in.

Trinity Mashup

Our Double, who toil in heaven,
Fire-burn be thy name.

Kingdom come and cauldron bubble
on earth as in fenny snake.

Give us this day our woolly bat
and forgive us our dog tongue

as we forgive those lizards
who blind-worm sting against us.

And lead us not
into charms
of powerful trouble,

but deliver us
from hell-broth
boil and bubble.

Berries, late summer

Spiny detritus surrounds the wild
Himalayan blackberry, everything
leading up to the fruit
an expression of spike and bristle.

Tiny hairs poke between
each purse of seed
that ruptures and stains
your thorn-pricked fingers.

The juice in your blood,
your blood on the berry
that we shape into free-form
pies. Bite-sized. Palmed.

Your hand cupped
over the bony rise
of my pelvis—

September
and all her sharpness
waning.

First Kill

I positioned myself to the right of the bird,
partly to block the view of the other chickens
watching from their tractor,
partly because I am right-handed
and needed to thrust forward with the knife.

Its body nestled in an upside-down cone,
the head dangled helplessly as I pulled the neck taut,
pointed the tip in front of the spine and
forced myself to drive the blade deep, a sickening
grizzle of metal through feathers and flesh.

Dogs shake a bird to addle its brain.
Eagles drop their prey, letting gravity
finish the kill. I used a knife and my hands
then watched the blood drain pink
as rubies or raspberry syrup.

That afternoon a colony of carpenter ants
swarmed the house. Thousands dotted
the siding and eaves, while in the backyard caterpillars
strangled the branch ends of every deciduous tree:
dogwood and gingko and plum. Robins raided the garden

and even hummingbirds dive-bombed the heads
of those who ventured too close. I stood back
as far as I could from the feeder, and forced myself
not to think how red its nectar was,
how slowly it drained—how rare and how sweet.

The Tao of Now

I.
In this land called now,
whatever's happening is always happening
till the crest of the next now
brings its own, infinite forever.
Just now, for example,
the cat purrs as he always purrs,
as the land of now dictates,
the purring that knows
no other moment,
no other state.

I.
But now,
in the now after now,
he cleans his paw,
tongue scraping
across the ever-terrain of his fur.

I.
And now,
in the now that is now
… purring…
as he always purrs,
humming and purring along,
as it is now.

I.
There are no ellipses in now.
Not now.
Unless one is waiting,
as one has always waited.
But why wait for now?
There is no point,
and that is exactly the point,
the point that is

now, the now-point in time
that is precisely this point
in time, is every point
in time, and why be
about the business of forever
making points now if
there really are no points now
but always this always
that is now.

I.
In the land that is now,
there are no question marks,
only unanswered questions.
There are no periods,
for periods imply
a period of—a passing of—time
a before and after
and a coming to an end
but there is no end to now
no comma colon semicolon exclamation mark
only the exclamation of now
marking now
and the purring
and the ohming
and the forever and the
cat next to us and the bird he dreams
and the blanket and the air
we breathe and the running
ribbon of thought and the body
we forgot is here
but we are all here now
forever writing
thinking
the words and the ink and the page

forever reading our way
across the ink here
and here and here
the here of now
the cat purring
now in the now
we know is ever
and ever will be
now

Horseshoe Highway

There's a barn on Horseshoe Highway, where every season the owner mounts
lights.
In spring a bunny, in fall a pumpkin. Come December, he usually puts up a star,
but this year he erected an angel with wide skirt, broad arms, and an unnaturally
tiny head.
Driving by late to catch the last ferry, I wonder about small-minded, pin-headed
angels.

The sweep of the Douglas fir branches, with their dip of vestments and upturned
tips,
follows exactly the encompassing curvature of angel arms that, even on an
indifferent
night like tonight, beckon, because now it's January. The war limps on.
Christmas and its attendant love-thy-neighbor have passed. In fact, there are no
neighbors

out tonight. Only me worried for the dumb angels, and noticing how the debris
from three solid days of wind makes beds of needles and cedar fronds
on the forest floor for the three-legged deer I've seen in these woods, and the
raccoon
whose eyes shine at night, and the Douglas squirrel who, good soldier that he is,

barks when frightened to warn the other squirrels. But none of it is real.
Not the angels, nor the loving arms of trees, nor the beds they create for furry
friends.
Even the compassion I feel is nothing more than a clever selfishness to trick me
into thinking 'I care therefore I am,' an undeserved elevation, a reaching toward
heaven,

like the tops of trees. A funny thing about the Doug fir: sometimes it bends a little,
so it doesn't reach its full height and certainly can't aspire to eternity.
As though it bumped its head against life's limits. Or perhaps was bowed down
like the cedar, dejected at the broken promise of life divine. I want to believe

the angel's head is small on purpose, so it won't accidentally lift itself into heaven,
but will stay on earth for those of us who need grace most. But this is the
    foolishness
of limited minds: the fearful and superstitious, those of us stubbornly unwilling to
    fall
like needles and boughs. Forgive me. I don't mean to sound unfeeling. It's January.

The roadside reflects more brown than green, and what little green remains
will turn brown soon enough. I'm just trying to catch a ferry. Not thinking about
    angels
staple-gunned to the sides of barns. Not thinking about fallen arms. Not thinking
how we're all nothing more than the future stomping grounds of rodents and the
    lame,

and maybe this is the most perfect, most just reward,
that we should lay our bodies into the loam for the limping deer
whose leg we hit on a night unbearably similar to tonight.

FOR THAT SLOW CRAFTED BARGAIN WITH TIME

Yellow Sea

"My heart is turning to ashes."
Chung Hae-Sook, waiting to hear news of her 16-year-old son
after a ferry from Incheon, South Korea, sank in the Yellow Sea.

Her heart curves, spinning toward slag.

The bones calcify as her legs scuttle
the broken hull of her hips, stranded and listing.

Her eyes leak a sallow sea.

Her throat, that long, strafed corridor of sorrow,
clenches and fists lumps of ashen lye.

She knows her son's legs drift like tree limbs

that once sifted the wind over *Incheon's* "wise river,"
where a swirl of apricot petals surges to sea.

Soon his jaw will hinge an unhurried song of April,

and seaweed will drape and finger the cold currents
where ashes eddy all our salt-water hearts.

Their Car the Day After

Grief avalanched at the smell of iron.
Potato chips everywhere, and something like dip
splotched throughout the car's interior.
I wiped a daub from my niece's backpack.
Gray matter, it turns out,
feels creamy like hummus or brie.
Speak to me of glaciers,
of rust's labor
and the crumble of granite.
Tell me about anything but the crush
of acceptance, that slow-crafted bargain
with time. I gaped at the backpack,
their beach towels, my jeans—
unsure what to do now with my hands.

Out Like a Lamb

I. Orcas Island

The men behind me say there is no god. We're waiting
for the ferry, about a dozen of us, in the Orcas Hotel Café,
while a windstorm and downpour conjure images of Noah.
Mother Teresa denounced god on her deathbed,
the man says. *The church covered it up.*

A former madam strolls in. Her oversized glasses magnify her seeing.
We live on an island of exiles, it's true. The man's voice continues.
Mother Teresa said, "There is no god. There is no heaven."
(Days later, Wikipedia tells me the nun at her bedside
claimed she had said, *I love you, Jesus, I love you, Jesus.*)

M, did you ever consider doing a little business here? At the hotel?
the other man asks. M points and says *the big guy upstairs*
—not God, but the owner—tossed the idea around. But she's kidding, right?
Or is she? My mother believed in legalizing prostitution. I just want to believe
in my fairytale island. I board the ferry, but cannot escape my own exile of faith.

II. Mainland

75 mile-per-hour winds. I'm driving 70 miles-per-hour myself
down I-5, listening to Muse, musing on March weather,
when I pass a broken-down Chevy, a woman wrapped in fleece,

and a man with a gas can walking against the wind.
I'm sorry, but I just have to ask, the woman says as they
bundle into my car, *are you a believer? In Jesus Christ?*

The wipers swipe. No. I tell her. I'd like to. But I doubt.
Her smile flatlines. Maybe she, too, wants to trust
that this savior was sent by her other Savior.

Maybe we're both wrong.

III. Everett

We drop off her boyfriend,
to find a mechanic.
Could I please take Melanie
to their apartment
a few more exits south?

Everett where my mother's oncologist
told her the cancer in her liver
was untreatable.

She has a two-year-old son,
and confesses she hasn't lost
the weight yet, confesses
she climbed on the scale
and it stopped at 309.

Everett where we filled Mom's
first morphine prescription,
and she got cash back.

That was a month ago,
and she's already lost
seven pounds. The doctor
told her to eat proteins
and walk 10,000 steps each day.

Everett where we stopped somewhere
for lunch—
why can't I remember?

I can drop her off here, she says,
she'll walk the rest of the way alone.
She glows with possibility.
I know you don't believe, but I just
have to say God bless you.

Where the trees had already turned yellow,
and Mom said God had a plan for us all
then patted my arm as I drove

Melanie shuts the door before I can
say goodbye, or explain the tears
brimming. *God bless you, too,*
I say to her empty seat. A swipe
across the windshield and eyes, as I slip

into nothingness and traffic.

The Light at the End of the Solar System

When the first photos of Pluto came hurtling
3 billion miles across the solar system,
everyone marveled at the surface texture—
scarred, like acid-etched granite, or leather
worried smooth in the galaxy's palm.

How carelessly Pluto sways, how torpid the days.

But this following the dream where my brother
emerged, months after his death. He packed
sticky notes and bottle openers from the kitchen
junk drawer, home of the lost and lonely. I stood
vacant in the doorway. *How? When?*

We've known for months, his wife said. *Didn't you
read it on Facebook?* Mark zipped up the box
in that easy way of large men, their grace in everyday
strokes. Ripping sound of the tape unspooling,
tearing against the serrated edge.

The lightspeed express from Pluto to Earth
takes 4-1/2 hours. What does it mean to die
in your sleep? How long does the dream unfurl
after the heart goes still? My brother owned two pet rats
who could squeeze through the bars of their cage
and escape to the cosmos of our basement.

Grief is Pluto in the palm: intangible, unimaginable,
ever-present, ever-gone. The junk drawer squeaks
like the exercise wheel spinning in the rats' cage.
There must be 3 billion ways not to open a kitchen drawer.
3 billion ways not to wake up.

Apologia

In those first days, when you were no more than a zygote
of haploid cells, I touched my fingertips to windowpanes
and listened for signs, the way the logs whispered
in the fire or how alder leaves scraped past
the screen door in a random, sweeping drift.
I tried to imagine your voice as an adult, a cross
between your father's and mine, and whether your nose

would dip when you talked or have an upturn
into ostentatiousness, but neither of these things happened—
other eventualities elbowed them aside,
like the time you defended yourself on the playground
and got hauled off to the principal's office. My fault,
I tried to explain. I was the one who egged him
to deck the next bully who shoved him around.

The fist in his hand matches his mother's, an inheritance
of stubborn righteousness that cannot be excised
the way his father and I excised ourselves from each other's lives.
Blame me, not the boy, I told them, but you still
got kicked out of school. The bible was only half right
on that sins of the father business, and only half wrong
on repent and ye shall be saved.

Light Soaks into the Landscape

In the moon-stained morning
I fill the kettle in near darkness,
turn the knob on the gas
till the flame erupts in blue,

casting shadows of my cup
and knuckles spilling
across the counter and wall.

I have no legacy to bequeath you,
only these same aches your grandmother
left me. A rooster crows in the distance.
Foghorns warn ships.

What do we know of each other,
of anyone really, but the mournful peal
of caution and hello.

When light soaks into the landscape
of your tomorrow, when your mother
has made herself one with the ground,
hold up this foghorn like a conch to your ear,

and know we are all bowed by the lone,
sometimes daunting, often exhilarating
eventuality of coil and bloom.

Favorite Theater

Where the wool velvet nap had worn thin,
horsehairs poked through the coarse weave.
Small chips chinked but did not detract
from the grace of mahogany seatbacks.

A pimply faced usher stood near the screen
saying *enjoy your drinks, relax, put your feet up.*
Elegant old theater, past its glory,
beyond, in that kid's eyes, restoring.

And so was our marriage, I guess.
It's been so long, I don't remember
the film. Afterward, we ate dessert
in the outdoor café. Warm Tucson breeze.

We would have talked about the movie.
Not like years later, when we left the courthouse
to a wan September sun, then shared sidewalk
drinks in Seattle's Pioneer Square.

Table dusty from road grime, the plastic-covered chairs
unyielding beneath us. We clinked glasses to our futures
as tourists waited in line for the underground tour
regaling those halcyon days before the great fire.

Moulting

The polished bones
of Madrona branches
burst through red casings
that peel off in sheets
like snake-skin
or the discarded husk
of that first marriage,
whose memory we sheathe,
surprised to admit
we sometimes
remember it
fondly.

All the King's Horses

In the reckoning of sins, we dredge through the till
of our own glacial drift. Your thrown coffee
cup, my dissatisfied pout. A stockpile
of accusations overflowing the dining table,
mantelpiece, and bed of our conjugal love.
Love, of course, said
                                        with an over-the-shoulder smirk.
Who knew winter with her ice shards and bared limbs
could outlast us both? Who knew we were not
each other's parents, never each other's kids. *I only wanted*
to protect you, I can hear you say. *I only wanted you*
to be happy, I return.
                                          When the clock
strikes *Forgiveness*, I'll meet you at the door
of that theater of the festering heartache. Bring your Yogi Bear
imitation, I'll bring my Elmer Fudd. When the clock strikes
We-Can-Laugh-About-It-Now, please, save a seat for me.

TO EASE OUR LOSS DOWN GENTLY

Honey, it's raining something terrible

Waiting inside Best Buy for a downpour
of biblical immensity to subside, I phone
not because I miss you, but because I can't bear

to think about the look on the face of the policeman
who comes in hatless and soaked,
how he wipes rain from an 8 x 10 frame

before showing it to the store greeter
who shakes his head no.
Nor can I describe the face in the picture

of the eleven or twelve year old boy, cheeks
round, skin flushed, and eyes whole.
Instead I say how the rain comes down in sheets,

how the pavement roils and lightning makes
random stabs at us all.
The policeman tries to shield the boy's face

as he runs to the next store.
After he leaves, I watch how, discomposed,
the greeter tries to ignore the paper

with basic facts and phone number in red,
the way he squeezes his eyes closed,
and how slowly he shakes his head.

Alula

To ease his landing
the eagle extends
elbow and carpal joints,
spreads his phalanges
and thrusts open his alula
like a thumb on the wing
as he drops against the captured air.

All summer we watched a mated pair
ride thermal columns
as they hunted field mice, rabbits, voles.

A fall wind storm loosened their aerie
perched in a crag
across the valley. Our neighbor
found the nest where it had landed
upright in a bed of salal.
Curious to see remnants of the roost,
maybe feathers or confetti of eaglet shells,

he found instead the stripped bones
of the eagles' prey,
along with collars, still in place.
Metal charms listed Fluffy, Buddy, Rollo
dozens of other pets
we'd seen on flyers all over town.

After the shock of it,
we made the easy comparisons,
marveling at the anatomy of wings,
their agile similarity to human hands,
and how, though we lack alulas,
we know full well
the callous dexterity of hunger
and opposable thumbs.

The truth we cannot admit,
though we turn away from jokes about poor Cupcake, poor Muffin,
is that we would give anything,
maybe even these thumbs
carrying cardboard caskets, shovels, and gloves,
to be able to ease our loss down gently,
wings aloft,
buffered by the calming air.

Writing the Beloved

Cartographer's pen
a relief map of pining

I surf state leap
too far, too tremble

What honey tincture trailing
What fresh root finding

Afterthought of soil speak
at window casement budge

Somewhere a moon
quiver-star in hover

Face these mountains wildly
I wait the other side

Sea Urge from Nebraska

How I miss our North Shore walks,
with bull kelp and sea lettuce drying on the rocks,
remnants of crab shells after plovers feed.

Each May, Coast Tsimshian sun-bake seaweed.
They press purple laver, rockweed, and porphyra
into cakes for inland friends. In four days I can reach you

by car, though I started my walk months ago. Sea
lavender under the pillow, I step closer in my dreams.
Gather with me the cedar limbs anchored in shallows

where herring eggs and sea palm lodge in hollow mesh.
We'll drape madrona branches with the drying boughs,
then remind the children not to pluck the rain flowers—

red columbine and bluebells—blooming in the mallow. We'll listen
for the hesh-hesh-hesh of teeth shredding sea grass. We'll swim
through eelgrass meadows, wring heat from bonfire flames,

and I'll no longer miss those North Shore walks,
how your fingers cradle gifts of sea glass
nestled in mussel shells coupled with byssal threads,
the way the sweat of sea salt lingers on my stomach and legs.

Askance

Satin trim slanks down my side
of the bed and the sheet
twists itself sideways
as we plank the covers
across the plain of our morning.

Today everything
runs perpendicular
to our passions:
the hour, the bedclothes,
my pettiness, your apology.

Wrong times at right angles.
The mood and moment amiss
as the cat paws the window
for one of us to open
every fastened lip and sash.

Before the Solstice

after the rain,
a thin stream trickles
along the downspouts. You stir
the covers, ear cocked
for the trickle of water
running. *Did someone leave*

the faucet on? Last night
I woke to find you gone.
Just sleeping on the sofa,
but this after you'd caressed
my arm, and I half asleep
thought you wanted me

to waken. Yet when I reached for
you, you turned away.
Daylight arrives before morning,
it flickers through a gap in the curtain
like you back into our bed.
Outside everything glistens.

Inside we shield our eyes
against what we forgot
to appreciate: these long days
before they diminish
to nothing, this brilliance
now gleaming off our lives.

North Beach, Low Tide

When for a minute or ten of our stretch of a walk
on beach and rocks spread like dark eggs
wet under barnacles and broken shells, when the sun
slipped beneath a point low
                                        on the bent horizon
of Saturna and Pender Islands, and the below-
sides of clouds flushed in foggy shades the tint
of yellowed paper or the last calendula, bristled
by northerly winds,
                                        we spotted a split pear
of basalt and granite, pink on one half,
near-black on the other, sky and horizon a smear
of ice cream and mud, and you said, *We're overdue
for the big one,*
            a seismic event and tsunami,
nine-point-oh on the Richter, and the whelp
of a seal barked or was it a heron. *I love you,* I said,
and the seaweed smelled of tumbling and smelt.

Kitchen Waltz

We tilled our garden beds, making way for heirloom starts,
cuddled into careful impressions. The peppers we staggered,
left to right, front to back, and they did, in a way, resemble dance steps,

instructional patterns for those less nimble, like me.
I questioned the wisdom of eggplant near sunflower. He questioned
my carelessness: the brush against chickweed, launching seeds

into startled orbit. But then I brushed him, or he grazed me,
and we gathered sprays of rosemary, marjoram, thyme,
and a quiver of chives before stepping inside.

Something happened next in the kitchen, the alchemy of lovers,
where food as primeval as catfish finds sesame oil and tikka masala,
scallions and pecans. Greens melted in the pan, then on our tongues,

like our muscles later in bed. I doubt either of us dreamt of dancing,
but one of us said, "Turn," in our sleep. Loud enough to wake us both,
but not so loud we could tell who had spoken. Two cooks,

one mind. A drowsy shifting under the covers. Two forks entwined.
A stomach pressed against a back, the other stomach unbridled and breathing.
I thought of quail—savory, delicate, and buttery—with fresh sage and arugula.

Winter Letter

I propped the envelope
wide on the potting bench
to catch the clean scent
reflected off snow.

When sealing for mail,
the trick lies in not
fanning these moments
thrushing back like birds‘ wings
into the crowded day.

The snow is so young
its light bleaches everything
brighter. I had to ink
your address last
so morning wouldn‘t wash
your whereabouts away.

When you gather my letter,
it may appear
empty as an envelope,
a missive lighter than air,
but open it,
gingerly now,
and breathe.

GRATITUDE

For invaluable feedback and encouragement on these poems, thanks goes to Jonis Agee, Grace Bauer, Marvin Bell, Norris Carlson, Kevin Clark, Stephen Corey, Lana Hechtmann Ayers, David Huddle, Ingrid Karnikis, Adrian Koesters, Ted Kooser, Carole Levin, JoEllen Moldoff, Michelle Reed, Stan Rubin, Tina Schumann, Michael Schmeltzer, Peggy Shumaker, John Sibley Williams, Dorothy Trogden, and Ed Wilson.

Much gratitude to family members Walter and Katheryn Toxey, Anne Parmley Toxey, Patrick McMillan, and Julia, Mark, Nicholas and Kate Agostini for their support of a walking and writing retreat in France, where many of these poems were first written.

Thank you to the A.P. Anderson Center, The Center for Great Plains Studies, PLAYA, Brush Creek Foundation for the Arts, Carol Owens and Bob Wyatt, and Anne and Shirish Mulherkar for their gifts of time, space, and support.

I'm grateful to the editors and staff at Finishing Line Press for their tireless commitment to publish fine literature, and for the care they've taken in bringing these poems to light.

A special thank you goes to Steve Escame, an extraordinary teacher, coach, and human being who will ever be an example of the finest in personal integrity and compassion.

Jill McCabe Johnson's first poetry collection, *Diary of the One Swelling Sea* (MoonPath, 2013), won the Nautilus Silver Award in Poetry. Much of her second poetry book, *Revolutions We'd Hoped We'd Outgrown* (Finishing Line, 2016), was written as Johnson trekked across France prior to and during the 2015 Daesh attacks on Paris, and explores the personal and political upheavals we all face. *Borderlines*, a nonfiction chapbook, was published by Sweet Publications in 2016. As series editor for the University of Nebraska Gender Programs, Johnson has edited the anthologies *Becoming: What Makes a Woman* (2012), and *Being: What Makes a Man* (2015), exploring voices across the spectrum of gender expression. Honors include an Artist Trust grant, an Academy of American Poets Award, the Mari Sandoz Prairie Schooner Prize in Fiction, plus the Deborah Tall Memorial Fellowship from Pacific Lutheran University, where she completed her MFA in Creative Writing, and the Louise Van Sickle Fellowship in Poetry from the University of Nebraska, where she received her PhD in English. Her writing has appeared in publications such as *Brevity, Defunct, Harpur Palate, Iron Horse Literary Review, The Southeast Review,* and *The Los Angeles Review.* Johnson is the founding director of Artsmith, a non-profit to support the arts, providing artist residencies, workshops, and retreats where she lives with her husband in the San Juan Islands.

BOOKS BY JILL MCCABE JOHNSON

Revolutions We'd Hoped We'd Outgrown
Diary of the One Swelling Sea
Borderlines
Becoming: What Makes a Woman
Being: What Makes a Man

CPSIA information can be obtained
at www.ICGtesting.com
Printed in the USA
FFOW03n1715280117
31850FF